IMAGES
of America

PASADENA
1940–2008

ON THE COVER: Pasadena's aquatic past holds mixed memories for many older Pasadena residents. In 1947, the Pasadena Department of Recreation had this photograph printed of a swim class at John Muir High School in response to an ongoing battle over desegregation of Pasadena's Brookside pool. The pool, integrated by court order in 1947, is an apt metaphor for Pasadena's modern history: a past filled with good times and bad, deserving of both pride and regret. (J. Allen Hawkins Collection.)

IMAGES
of America

PASADENA
1940–2008

Patrick Conyers, Cedar Phillips, and
the Pasadena Museum of History

ARCADIA
PUBLISHING

Published by Arcadia Publishing
Charleston, South Carolina

Library of Congress Control Number: 2008942859

For all general information contact Arcadia Publishing at:
Telephone 843-853-2070
Fax 843-853-0044
E-mail sales@arcadiapublishing.com
For customer service and orders:
Toll-Free 1-888-313-2665

Visit us on the Internet at www.arcadiapublishing.com

This book is dedicated to the volunteers, staff, trustees, and members of the Pasadena Museum of History, past and present.

CONTENTS

ACKNOWLEDGMENTS

The reader will notice that the majority of the images reproduced in this book are part of the permanent collection of the Pasadena Museum of History. The photographic collection at the museum is substantial, historically significant, and (thankfully) available to the general public as well as to professional researchers. We have relied most heavily on two specific photographic collections, the J. Allen Hawkins Collection and the *Pasadena Star-News* Collection. Both of these collections were essential to our ability to tell Pasadena's engrossing history properly. We are grateful to Karen Craig, president of the board of trustees, and executive director Jeanette L. O'Malley for their willingness to open the collections for this book. An especial debt of gratitude is owed to Laura Verlaque, collections manager, for her generous and patient help, and to museum volunteer Bob Bennett, who spent countless laborious hours pulling photographs and scanning them for us as well as offered his keen editing eye and invaluable advice. Thank you to Katie Brandon and Michelle Turner for help tracking down photographs we just had to have in the book. Thanks are owed to many others who live and work in Pasadena. To Terry LeMoncheck, Steve Nowlin, Joan Palmer, Rochelle Branch, and Pauline Kamiyama, thank you for your help in assembling photographs that tell the story of recent Pasadena. Patrick appreciates Russ Palmer and Gene Moscarat sharing their stories of Consolidated Engineering Corporation (CEC), and Jon Cohn for offering to help, even though he lives in Glendale. Thank you to the University of Minnesota, home to the Charles Babbage Institute Collection and ElectroData Company papers, useful sources of information for Pasadena's technological heritage. A hearty and wholehearted thank-you goes to our fantastic editor, Jerry Roberts. Finally, and most importantly, Patrick would like to thank his wife, Angela, for her love and support, and to little Leo and Mira as well. Cedar thanks her husband, Andrew, and son, Jackson, for their willingness to listen to countless anecdotes from modern Pasadena history, as well as for their love and support in this and other ventures.

INTRODUCTION

Modern Pasadena, defined here as the years following 1940, has seen many changes over the decades. World War II, postwar prosperity, the cold war, the civil rights movement, urban renewal, and more modern urban revitalization have shaped the city's identity.

The 1940s brought the end of the Great Depression and the beginning of a world war. Families watched their loved ones go off to fight while local Japanese American citizens had the hardship of forced relocation to government-run internment camps. World War II affected everyone in Pasadena, regardless of individual circumstances. The local economy saw some benefit, with local scientific and manufacturing companies earning lucrative war-related government contracts.

The years following World War II transformed Pasadena into the epitome of the mid-20th-century California dream city, with new homes popping up on lots dotted with citrus and avocado trees. The automobile took center stage in this new world, with developments featuring plentiful and free parking for all.

While the postwar boom years were filled with promise and opportunity for many, Pasadena was far from perfect. Race and ethnicity-based housing restrictions limited the options of nonwhite residents. While the city was home to an ethnically diverse population, segregation and outright racism were unfortunate facts of life.

The 1960s brought with it the civil rights movement. In Pasadena, the struggle for equality culminated in the *Spangler v. Pasadena Board of Education* court case. The case, filed by Jim and Bobbie Spangler, Skipper and Pat Rostker, and Wilton and Dorothy Clarke, attempted to force the integration of Pasadena's schools. Although the U.S. District Court decided in the Spangler's favor, a later decision by the U.S. Supreme Court rolled back many of the dictates of the original decision. In a city filled with glorious moments, it remains one of its greatest shames that its school district was the only one outside of the American South to be forcibly desegregated by decree of the federal government.

The 1970s was an era of massive urban renewal projects and goals, some successful and others not. The Pasadena Civic Auditorium was expanded to a full-scale convention center, complete with hotel, parking, and exhibition space. Today it remains a top performance venue and has hosted famous events such as the Emmy Awards, the People's Choice Awards, and American Idol. Unfortunate projects included the demolition of the Pasadena Athletic Club and other historic properties to make space for the unsuccessful Plaza Pasadena.

Things started to change yet again in the 1980s. Thanks in part to an urban "renewal" backlash, a historic preservation movement began to gain traction. The public became increasingly interested in Pasadena's craftsman homes, as well as in its historic civic and commercial buildings. Rather than seeing Pasadena's past as dusty relics, these new preservationists saw in them the potential for better and more far-reaching community revitalization than the destructive urban renewal policies of the previous decades. Pasadena Heritage, founded in 1977, took on an active role in the preservation of Pasadena's diverse historic built environment.

The 1990s saw Old Pasadena begin to recover some of its historic luster, once again luring Pasadenans to their historic downtown core for shopping, dining, and working. The One Colorado development in the heart of Old Pasadena won national acclaim and played an instrumental role in the continued revitalization of the downtown neighborhood.

Pasadena during the 1990s also faced ongoing problems with crime in some areas, the worst of it gang related. The infamous Halloween Homicides, the deadly shooting of three children leaving a Halloween party, led incoming Pasadena police chief Barney Melekian to promise "no more dead kids," a pledge that was to become the department's unofficial motto. New social programs, particularly those with the goal of helping local youth, as well as an aggressive gang task force, helped to bring down the violent crime rate by the end of the decade.

Pasadena in the 2000s has seen the continued gentrification of the core downtown, as well as the redevelopment of other areas along the Colorado Boulevard commercial corridor. The 2003 Paseo Colorado development, located at Colorado Boulevard and Los Robles Avenue, transformed the shell of the former Plaza Pasadena, an enclosed shopping mall, into an indoor-outdoor shopping and dining destination, complete with a grocery store and apartments.

Throughout recent history, some things have remained constant. The world-famous Tournament of Roses Parade and Rose Bowl Game continue to be held each January, both longtime Pasadena events that have become treasured family traditions in many households. Pasadena's outdoor spaces and parks continue to provide opportunities for local residents to fully take advantage of Southern California's balmy climate. Its schools, including the California Institute of Technology, the Art Center of College and Design, the Fuller Theological Seminary, and the Pasadena City College, train future local, regional, and national innovators and leaders. The local arts and culture scene, a part of Pasadena since its earliest years, continues to contribute to the city's quality of life.

Unless otherwise noted, the photographs in this book come from the extensive photograph archives at the Pasadena Museum of History. The Pasadena Museum of History is dedicated to preserving and sharing the history and culture of this area, from its early days through the present. These images are only a small taste of the museum's holdings, just as they represent only a small fraction of Pasadena's rich and varied past.

One

THE WAR YEARS AND BEYOND
1940s

The 1940s was a pivotal decade for Pasadena, as it was for the rest of the country. The beginning of the decade brought with it the end of the Depression as well as the country's entrance into World War II. Many Pasadenans joined the military, while others contributed to the war effort through their military-related scientific research. Both the California Institute of Technology (Caltech) as well as the Jet Propulsion Laboratory worked on war-related projects, as did a number of related technical businesses.

World War II had perhaps its greatest local impact on Pasadena's Japanese American community. Starting in March 1942, the nearby Santa Anita Racetrack held local Japanese Americans until they were moved to government-run internment camps. Families were forced to leave behind their homes and businesses, bringing with them only what they could carry.

The end of World War II ushered in a new American period of prosperity and expansion. Pasadena's economic base shifted with the times, moving away from tourism and agriculture toward technology and light industry. Former citrus and grape fields were transformed into neighborhoods filled with homes for returning soldiers and their families. New retail and industrial centers popped up in east Pasadena and in the Hastings Ranch area. Pasadena's traditional shopping district, the area around Fair Oaks Avenue and Colorado Boulevard, lost its luster as the city's premier shopping area moved toward more automobile-friendly modern developments along South Lake Avenue.

Pasadena remained a diverse city, but residents of different ethnic groups lived mostly segregated lives due, in part, to race-based housing restrictions.

In February 1925, Pasadena sought to bring a southern branch of the University of California (UC) to the city and locate it in the then-undeveloped Hastings Ranch area. The committee that made the petition to the UC regents was a "who's who" of Pasadena, including Caltech's Robert Millikan and George Ellery Hale of the Mt. Wilson Observatory. Pasadena was one of three finalists, but the regents decided to locate the new university—now UCLA—in Westwood instead. In 1941, when this photograph was taken, the land remained undeveloped. (Photograph by Robert Spence, Spence Air Photos.)

The Pasadena Civic Orchestra, shown here in 1940, was founded in 1928 by conductor Reginald Bland. In 1940, the Civic Orchestra was a mix of professional and amateur musicians. They worked under music director and conductor Dr. Richard Lent, a German conductor who came to the United States in the 1930s due to the political unrest at home. The Pasadena Civic Orchestra lives on today as the Pasadena Symphony.

This is the 1944 Washington Junior High varsity football team, coached by Don Shoup. They were the 1A champions that year.

Pasadena's Union Pacific Depot was originally built in 1904 for the San Pedro, Los Angeles, and Salt Lake Railroad, and was later purchased by Union Pacific in 1921. It was located at 205 West Colorado Boulevard. Service to the station ended in the late 1960s when the freeway was built. The exterior (pictured above) and the interior (shown below) were photographed in June 1945.

The students in Miss Lickmor's Longfellow Elementary School were photographed here in 1948. The school is still in operation and is located at 1065 East Washington Boulevard. These young students, born during the early 1940s, would soon be followed by the aptly named baby boomer generation.

In May 1946, the Los Angeles area was chosen to host the country's first experiment with helicopter airmail. Two helicopters were scheduled to make twice daily circuits from the Los Angeles Municipal Airport to Pasadena, Glendale, Pomona, Santa Monica, Long Beach, and others cities en route. This photograph is of one such helicopter—likely on a promotional tour—landing near city hall on July 8, 1946. (J. Allen Hawkins Collection.)

Percy Carter Jr. posed for this 1944 photograph at South Fair Oaks Avenue and Green Street. The Carter family owned and operated the Carver Hotel, the first local hotel owned and operated by African Americans. It was located in the Doty Block at 103–115 South Fair Oaks Avenue and was also home to the Onyx Club, which played host to many famous jazz musicians during the 1940s and 1950s. (Black History Collection.)

Naomi Bowen of Pasadena strikes a pose for the camera on West Dayton Street around 1944. West Dayton Street holds an important place in local African American history; among other things, the street was home to the Francisco Building, the first Pasadena commercial building built by and for African Americans. In the 1940s, the street still housed many businesses owned and operated by Pasadena's black residents. (Black History Collection.)

Here an employee of the G. M. Giannini Company tests a model jet airplane at the Rose Bowl on May 8, 1946. The jet is in the photograph's upper left. Both American and Russian scientists learned substantial lessons from German V-2 rocket technology after the end of the European war. (Photograph by J. Allen Hawkins.)

On VE Day, May 8, 1945, Pasadenans took to the streets, in this case East Colorado Boulevard, to celebrate Germany's formal surrender. Pasadena was deeply involved in wartime activities. Its remaining grand hotels had been converted to military purposes, and the city was a center for war-related scientific research and manufacturing. (*Pasadena Star-News* Collection.)

In addition to athletic facilities, the Pasadena Athletic Club, located at Green Street and Los Robles Avenue, offered social activities and dining. During World War II, the U.S. Army turned the club's basement into a private club for area officers. In 1946, the army's space was converted into a nightclub for club members. This photograph, taken on Christmas Eve of that year, shows some of the club's hardworking staff. (J. Allen Hawkins Collection.)

The Green and Lake Café, located at 90 South Lake Avenue at the corner of Green Street and Lake Avenue, was photographed here in October 1946. South Lake Avenue was on the cusp of major changes. In 1947, Bullock's Department Store would open just down the street, and Lake Avenue south of Colorado Boulevard would become the shopping and eating destination of choice for fashionable Pasadenans. (J. Allen Hawkins Collection.)

This display at the Pasadena City Library, located at 285 East Walnut Street, enticed library patrons to read one of the featured books. *Anthony Adverse*, by Hervey Allen, was the highlight of this November 13, 1946, book table. The display and its books were sponsored by Pasadena's most famous bookstore, Vroman's. (J. Allen Hawkins Collection.)

Races like this "doodlebug" race on September 3, 1946, enjoyed a passionate following, including the photographer of this race, J. Allen "Al" Hawkins. Hawkins was a racing aficionado who had operated Al's Motor Shop from 1938 to 1945, during which time Hawkins estimated he built more than 4,000 race engines. (J. Allen Hawkins Collection.)

Pasadena police officer Ray Bartlett poses next to a burglar he arrested in 1948. Prior to his long and distinguished career in the Pasadena Police Department, Bartlett had been a successful college athlete and a decorated army veteran. He was only the second African American to join the city's police force. This particular arrest was a dramatic affair; note the bullet hole in the car and the safe in the trunk. (Black History Collection.)

This streetcar is pictured at the intersection of Fair Oaks Avenue and Walnut Street in February 1948. The bell tower of St. Andrew's Catholic Church, one of the most iconic pieces of architecture in Pasadena (built in 1927 and designed by Robert Montgomery), dominates the background. At one time, the Los Angeles area could boast the country's best public transportation, thanks largely to its extensive trolley system. (Pacific Electric Collection.)

On October 20, 1949, Rev. Max Morrison (sixth from left) and principal congregants of Westminster Presbyterian Church gathered to ceremonially burn the church's mortgage. The main building of the church was designed and built in 1927 by the firm of Marston, Van Pelt, and Maybury at a cost of $300,000. (J. Allen Hawkins Collection.)

Formed in 1942 in Pasadena, the Aerojet Corporation had already moved to Azusa by 1947, when this image was taken. Pictured is the manufacture of solid propellant Jet Assistant Take Off (JATO) units, designed to aid heavy aircraft to take off quickly. Aerojet was a pioneer in rocket technology, and it was founded by several of the principal actors in GALCIT (Guggenheim Aeronautical Laboratory at the California Institute of Technology), including GALCIT's first director, Theodore Von Kármán. (J. Allen Hawkins Collection.)

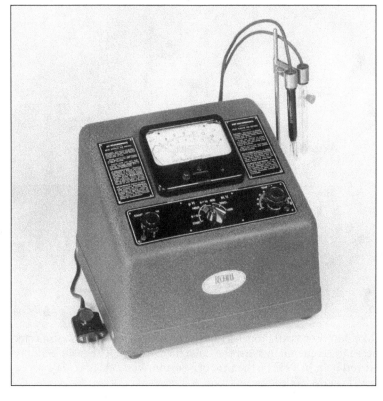

Arnold O. Beckman was, in Robert Millikan's grand understatement, "a most successful product of California Institute of Technology." Beckman founded the National Technology Laboratories in Pasadena. By 1948, when this PH meter was photographed, the company's home was on Mission Street in South Pasadena, a stop on its way to Fullerton. The company is today called Beckman-Coulter. (J. Allen Hawkins Collection.)

Hycon made a myriad of manufactured goods, from whipped cream dispensers to ordnance. Featured in this 1949 photograph is a strip camera. Hycon's founder, Trevor Gardner, who in February 1955 became assistant secretary of the U.S. Air Force, was fixated on the threat of Soviet missiles. He resigned that position in 1956 (a "pyrotechnical resignation," wrote the *Los Angeles Times*) to draw attention to the government's underfunding of the intercontinental ballistic missile (ICBM) program. (J. Allen Hawkins Collection.)

United Geophysical was started in 1935 by Herbert Hoover Jr. The company searched for oil by explosion-induced seismic waves. United Geophysical built machinery to record and analyze the results of those explosions—with the idea being that the resulting seismic waves would appear different if there were a space underground with lesser density than typical, identifying possible oil deposits. This photograph dates from 1949. (J. Allen Hawkins Collection.)

The Bullock's Department Store received national attention for its design; not only was the building itself notable, but so was its parking lot. The parking lot, photographed here on the store's opening day, September 10, 1947, was a full six acres and was intended to be the store's primary entrance. Cities everywhere were changing, and Bullock's Pasadena represented a new era of automobile-driven development. (*Pasadena Star-News* Collection.)

The Bullock's Department Store in Pasadena opened in 1947. Both the store and the South Lake Avenue commercial strip were milestones in Pasadena's history. The act of opening a department store in a new, suburban shopping street instead of a more traditional downtown location is symbolic of Pasadena's—and America's—postwar suburban development. (Photograph by Mayard L. Parker, Modern Photography.)

Local architect Wallace Neff developed these distinctive "bubble houses" to provide aesthetically interesting yet affordable homes for the postwar housing market. They were created by coating a giant rubber-coated balloon with gunite and then covering the form with concrete. Neff built this 1946 house, located at 1097 South Los Robles Avenue, for his brother Andrew. This home is one of the few bubble houses still surviving.

On December 7, 1946, the Kilgore Rangers played the Compton Tartars in the first "Little Rose Bowl," the junior college "mythical" national championship. "Adding spice to the fracas," the *Los Angeles Times* promised, "will be the halftime performance of Kilgore's famed Rangerettes, 48 beauteous gals who strut through intricate precision drills and dances." Here the Rangerettes pose at a pregame event at the Pasadena Civic Auditorium ballroom (today the Pasadena Ice Skating Center) on December 5, 1946. (J. Allen Hawkins Collection.)

The employees of this car dealership on the northwest corner of Raymond Avenue and Green Street faced an unusual task when they had to clear three inches of snow from their stock following a January 11, 1949, storm. Pasadena drivers were not accustomed to driving in sleet and snow, and the city was unprepared to provide plowing or salting services. A county road grader was put into service as an emergency plow.

The January 1949 snowstorm transformed Pasadena's typical post–Tournament of Roses streetscape. This photograph was taken from the corner of Colorado and Orange Grove Boulevards and looks east along Colorado Boulevard toward downtown. The grandstands on the left had yet to be removed from the 1949 Tournament of Roses parade. (Photograph by William Hart.)

For most people, the snow of January 1949, the first in 17 years, was either an exciting novelty or a temporary nuisance. At Brookside Golf Course, golfers hit the links despite the snow, while at Pasadena Junior College, students made snowmen. Most schools remained open, with an impressive 60 percent of students in attendance. This photograph was taken on North Lake Avenue. (J. Allen Hawkins Collection.)

This boy was thrilled to open the window of his home at Del Mar Boulevard and South Los Robles Avenue in January 1949 to find his front yard covered with snow. It was not only children who found the snow exciting; Pasadena Police set up special patrols at the local colleges to discourage out-of-control snowball fights and snow-induced riots. (*Pasadena Star-News* Collection.)

Gabriel M. Giannini was a native Italian who escaped Mussolini's tyranny and immigrated to the United States before the start of World War II. Giannini was a successful businessman. His company, G. M. Giannini and Company (later Giannini Controls) did extensive jet-power testing and created instruments for army and navy guided missiles in the mid- to late 1940s. Giannini was one of a group of Italian scientists (including Enrico Fermi) that held the 1935 U.S. patent on atomic power (No. 2,206,634). The value of the patent was estimated as high as $10 million, but legal wrangling finally resulted in an August 1953 payout of $300,000 to the group, excepting Dr. Bruno Pontecorvo, who had vanished from Finland in 1950 and was presumed to be working for the Russians. (J. Allen Hawkins Collection.)

Two

PROSPERITY AND
EXPANSION
1950s

Pasadena in the 1950s saw the continuation of the new housing and economic trends started in the postwar period. Newer developments in Hastings Ranch and elsewhere continued to expand, while some older city neighborhoods began to deteriorate.

Pasadena's local economy continued to be heavily shaped by science and technology. Many local firms that had beaten plowshares into swords to aid the war effort continued to intertwine themselves in postwar America's military-industrial complex. But many technological breakthroughs made for the military had tremendous commercial potential as well. Improvements in petroleum refining, the development of ever more complex computer technology, rapidly intensifying experiments in jet technology, and many other Pasadena-based innovations directly contributed to the country's economic prosperity in the 1950s.

The city's retail and service economy benefited, too, with the boom in population (the city's population grew from roughly 82,000 in 1940 to 115,000 in 1960) and continued prosperity. Residents could do all their shopping locally, from department stores, to newly popular supermarkets, to more traditional "mom and pop" shops.

Pasadena's historic downtown, anchored by the Colorado Boulevard and Fair Oaks Avenue intersection, started to decline during this decade as commercial activity continued to move eastward. The disinterest in the area's older buildings actually paid dividends in later decades when the historic architecture was restored and brought back to life.

Shown here is an aerial view of Eaton's Restaurant and Motel, located at the southeast corner of Colorado Boulevard and Michillinda Avenue, around 1959. The hotel was short-lived; it closed in 1969 after failing to pay $42,000 in federal taxes. (J. Allen Hawkins Collection.)

Here is a photograph of Hastings Ranch from January 1953. This view shows the extensive development that had been completed since 1945. Following the 1942 death of owner Charles H. Hastings, the approximately 1000-acre ranch was sold in 1945 to a Los Angeles developer, John R. Murphy, for $1,175,000. Hastings had inherited his fortune from his father, a California forty-niner. (Photograph by Robert Spence.)

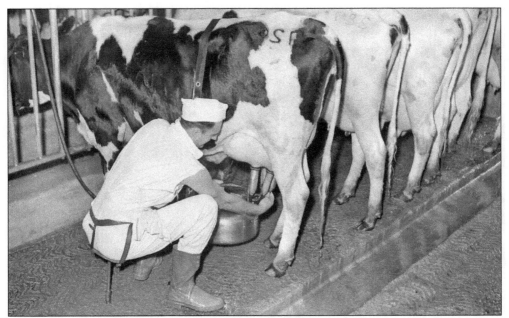

Much of Pasadena's agricultural pockets had been developed by the 1950s, although some elements remained. Supreme Dairy, a large local dairy founded in 1929, continued to flourish at its location at 2900 East Foothill Boulevard. In 1951, the year of this photograph, Supreme Dairy founder L. Clifford Kenworthy had the honor of serving as the president of the Tournament of Roses. (J. Allen Hawkins Collection.)

In June 1951, the Valley Maid Creamery commissioned this photograph, taken at Mar Vista Avenue and Colorado Boulevard, to celebrate its Driver of the Month, Oval Wylie. Presenting Wylie with a commemorative trophy is John Bentz. The photograph was to run as a paid advertisement in area newspapers. (J. Allen Hawkins Collection.)

One of Pasadena's streetcars waits at the corner of Fair Oaks Avenue and Del Mar Boulevard in March 1950. Pasadena, like the rest of the Los Angeles region, was well served by streetcars, making it possible for locals and visitors alike to travel from Pasadena to downtown Los Angeles, Hollywood, Santa Monica, or Long Beach, and to easily traverse the neighborhoods of Pasadena and neighboring communities. (Pacific Electric Collection.)

This view shows Colorado Street (present-day Colorado Boulevard) looking east from Broadway (today's Arroyo Parkway) in 1951.

J. Allen Hawkins captured this moment at the intersection of Hill Avenue and Colorado Street on May 22, 1951. Colorado Street was renamed Colorado Boulevard in 1958. (J. Allen Hawkins Collection.)

The Autoette electric car showroom was located at 250 North Lake Avenue. Autoettes were produced by Royce Steevers in Long Beach beginning in 1948. Production of the distinctive three-wheeled electric cars ended around 1970. This photograph was taken on March 21, 1955. (J. Allen Hawkins Collection.)

In 1958, the Pasadena Health Department, along with the National Polio Foundation and the Pasadena Medical Association, formed a program dedicated to ensuring that all Pasadena adults received their polio vaccination. The "polio for adults" drive kicked off with the vaccination of 36 city council members. City officials posed for this promotional photograph as a part of the vaccination effort. (J. Allen Hawkins Collection.)

J. Allen Hawkins captured this happy scene of a man, a woman, and a doll at a Pasadena Red Cross–run baby care class on January 26, 1951. (J. Allen Hawkins Collection.)

This is the graduating class of 1950 from the Mayfield School. Established in 1931 in Pasadena on South Euclid Avenue, the school's enrollment had grown sufficiently to necessitate expansion. Eight days after this photograph was taken, following three years of negotiation, the school bought 500 Bellefontaine Street, where a distinct senior school was opened that September. The white gowns and bouquets were school traditions. (J. Allen Hawkins Collection.)

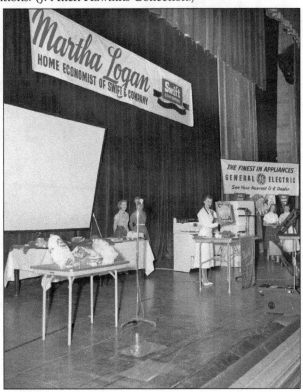

The *Pasadena Star-News* ordered this photograph of a cooking event taking place at the Pasadena Civic Auditorium on April 6, 1955. Martha Logan, the Swift and Company's home economist, had made a similar presentation the previous year and regaled the audience by making sausage spoon bread (a Southern recipe), corned beef brisket and accompanying chilled whipped cream and horseradish sauce, turkey a la queen, and butter-crisp fried chicken. (J. Allen Hawkins Collection.)

The July 21, 1952, Kern County earthquake was the largest to hit the continental United States since the 1906 San Francisco earthquake. The aftershocks from the magnitude 7.3 earthquake continued for quite some time. Caltech recorded 188 aftershocks of 4.0 or higher through September 26. Here two men replace broken window panels at Nelson's 5-10-25 Cent Store on North Lake Avenue in Pasadena. (*Pasadena Star-News* Collection.)

This building at the intersection of Fair Oaks Avenue and Union Street suffered some damage in the 1952 Kern County earthquake. (*Pasadena Star-News* Collection.)

The new 70,000-square-foot modern, scientific instrument plant built for Consolidated Engineering Corporation (CEC) is located in the center of this October 1951 photograph. The building's address was 300 North Sierra Madre Villa Avenue. Today, Bed Bath and Beyond sits on the former site of the CEC building, and the recently closed Hastings Theater on Rosemead Boulevard occupies the site where the Hastings Drive-In (upper left) was located. (J. Allen Hawkins Collection.)

A crane works to clear mud from Linda Vista Avenue after torrential rains set off mud slides across the Southland. At two points along Linda Vista, the *Los Angeles Times* reported in January 1952, "mounds of silt from the adjoining hilly region all but blocked the street to traffic." Hastings Ranch suffered even more severe mud slides and damage. (*Pasadena Star-News* Collection.)

South Lake Avenue was a well-established prime shopping destination by the 1950s. This photograph was taken in November 1959 and shows South Lake Avenue looking north from San Pasqual Avenue. Holiday shoppers flocked to both Bullock's Department Store, on the left, and Desmond's, on the right. Both stores provided free parking, as did the other shops lining the street.

Photographer J. Allen Hawkins's car is the focus of this 1959 photograph. Not content with the factory-built engine of this 1932 Ford Model B, Hawkins "hopped up" the car with a 1942 race engine. According to the July 1961 issue of *Meguiar's Sports Mirror*, in which Hawkins was named Sportsman of the Month, the car was "a familiar sight on Southland highways, carrying Al from assignment to assignment." (J. Allen Hawkins Collection.)

This 1955 advertisement created by the Pasadena Humane Society encouraged pet owners to request pet-care instructional brochures. The Pasadena Humane Society, according to *A Pasadena Chronology 1769–1977*, was started on October 18, 1894, "as an auxiliary to the Los Angeles group." (J. Allen Hawkins Collection.)

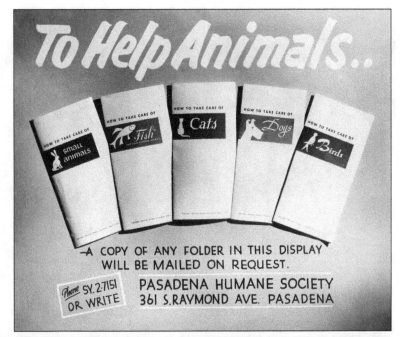

This boy admires a parrot and cage available for sale at Pasadena's Farmer's Market store in 1951, located at 200 North Lake Avenue. The Farmer's Market brought together different, independently owned departments under one roof, allowing shoppers to purchase everything from pets, to shoes, to groceries in one place. The Farmer's Market also promoted its "acres" of free parking, reflecting the rise of postwar suburban development. (J. Allen Hawkins Collection.)

Assembled here is some of the staff of the Consolidated Engineering Corporation at a banquet at the Huntington Hotel on May 18, 1951. They are seated in the hotel's Viennese Ballroom, its structure almost entirely masked by floor-to-ceiling draperies. The hotel is today known as the Langham, Huntington Hotel and Spa, Pasadena. (J. Allen Hawkins Collection.)

Herbert Hoover Jr., son of the 31st U.S. president, founded United Geophysical Company in 1935 and Consolidated Engineering Corporation in 1937. Both businesses were wildly successful, each eventually employing more than 1,000 people. He became undersecretary of state under U.S. president Dwight D. Eisenhower and was, for a time, considered Ike's heir apparent. Hoover died at Huntington Hospital in 1969 at the age of 65. (J. Allen Hawkins Collection.)

Located at 370 South Fair Oaks Avenue, and opened and operated by Fern A. Yarbrough, the American Microphone Company created mics used extensively in the television and motion picture industry. The D-22, pictured here in 1950, was described in advertisements as an "omnidirectional and dynamic microphone" that permitted "full vision styling for artist and audience." (J. Allen Hawkins Collection.)

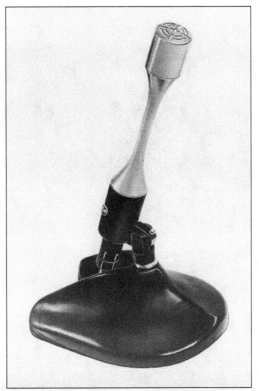

Francis L. Moseley established the F. L. Moseley Company in Pasadena in 1951. He is pictured here with one of his plotting recorders in March 1959. In 1958, the F. L. Moseley Company was acquired by Hewlett Packard—that company's first acquisition, and Moseley continued producing state-of-the-art recording instruments under the name Hewlett Packard Moseley Division. (J. Allen Hawkins Collection.)

Linus Pauling, two-time Nobel Prize winner, was photographed in November 1954 with a model of DNA. He was a professor of theoretical chemistry at Caltech, where, as described by the 1954 Nobel Prize committee, he conducted "research into the nature of the chemical bond and its application to the elucidation of the structure of complex substances." He is considered one of the greatest scientific minds of the 20th century. (J. Allen Hawkins Collection.)

ElectroData was created as a subsidiary of the Consolidated Engineering Corporation in 1954. After separating from CEC, the company was bought by Detroit's Burroughs Corporation in 1957. The year 1958 was an especially strong one for international sales. In December alone, $2.3 million worth of computers were sold from the company's plant at 460 Sierra Madre Villa Avenue. This model 205 computer departed for South Africa in August 1958. (J. Allen Hawkins Collection.)

Pictured here is the production of a radio show at KPPC (Pasadena Presbyterian Church) in Pasadena in 1951. The station was started in 1924 with meager signal strength and a modest schedule. It originally operated only Wednesday evenings and Sundays. The station's AM license was BR-34, meaning it was the 34th station licensed by the FCC. In May 1951, the station petitioned the FCC for a power boost from 100 to 250 watts but was denied. In 1962, the station began broadcasting on 106.7 FM and became a noted underground radio station from 1967 to 1971. Pete Johnson, a popular music columnist for the *Los Angeles Times*, commented on March 4, 1968, "Pasadena's KPPC . . . offer[s] palatable alternatives to AM rock programming, working primarily from an eclectic well-stocked album library." The FM station was sold in 1972 to KROQ; the AM station was sold in 1996. (J. Allen Hawkins Collection.)

Tom, Dick, and Harry O'Lear, six-year-old triplets from Arcadia, are pictured here watching the construction of the Iowa State float entry to the 1959 Tournament of Roses Parade. The triplets' names and coordinating jackets suggest their parents' penchant for attention. In August 1958, the triplets had crashed Chico Marx's wedding hoping to meet Harpo, a man, according to the *Los Angeles Times*, the boys both admired and resembled. (J. Allen Hawkins Collection.)

A celebration of the California Institute of Technology's 60th anniversary was held at the Huntington Hotel on November 9, 1951. Among the VIPs were Lee DuBridge (second from left), president of Caltech from 1946 to 1969, and his predecessor, Robert Millikan (second from right). The other men are unidentified. (J. Allen Hawkins Collection.)

Pictured here are congregants of Pasadena's Metropolitan Baptist Church in the 1950s. The church's Rev. John Cooper was a prominent civil rights leader in the 1960s and 1970s. As chairman of the Pasadena Black Convention, Cooper worked with the ACLU to pressure the city to amend board of director runoff election procedures that he felt were unfair to African American candidates. (J. Allen Hawkins Collection.)

This photograph was ordered by the William Wilson Company, a real estate brokerage. Shown is the northeast corner of Los Robles Avenue and Green Street on July 26, 1951. The Amalgamated Bank today occupies the corner where First Federal Savings of Pasadena had been. (J. Allen Hawkins Collection.)

Pasadena's second central library branch, located at East Walnut and Raymond Streets, was severely damaged in the Long Beach earthquake of 1933. The building was condemned soon afterwards but was not demolished until 1954 (pictured here). The city took pains to maintain the library's distinctive arch, which was later damaged in the Northridge earthquake of 1994.

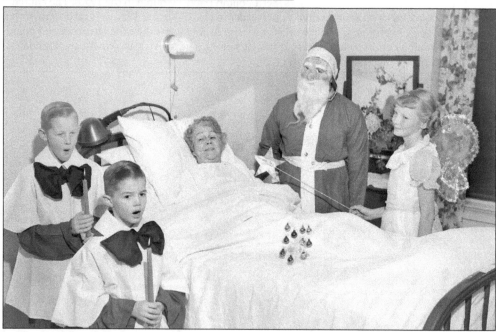

J. Allen Hawkins took several roving photographs at Huntington Hospital on November 28, 1950. Hawkins captured several scenes but none as interesting as this one, which features an unsettling incarnation of Father Christmas, an angel, and two carolers surrounding the bed of a patient. (J. Allen Hawkins Collection.)

Pioneer Bridge was dedicated in October 1953. Despite the 100-degree temperatures, people gathered to celebrate the opening with a parade and commemorative speeches. The bridge was named in honor of the original members of Pasadena's Indiana Colony, and many of their children and grandchildren were on hand to observe the ceremonies. The six-lane bridge was designed for regional automobile traffic and ran parallel to the older Colorado Street Bridge, which would carry lower levels of local traffic. At the time, it was the largest bridge built by the state of California. The *Pasadena Star-News* reporter covering the event enthused that the bridge would serve as "another link in the chain of the great metropolitan freeway system so urgently needed to serve the traffic needs of this populous and growing Southern California area." (Photograph by *Pasadena Star-News*.)

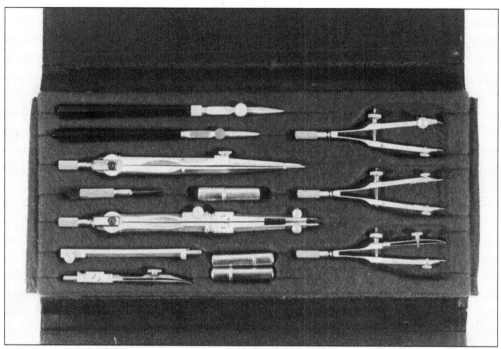

V&E Manufacturing began producing drafting instruments in Pasadena in 1939. Started by Francis E. Vaughan and Floyd Eubanks, the company came to be known as Vemco. Shown here is an assortment of precision drafting tools, photographed in 1950. (J. Allen Hawkins Collection.)

This is a code generator prototype, made by G. M. Giannini and Company and photographed in 1950. In addition to its early work on jet motor production, Giannini was subcontracted by the Douglas Aircraft Company to contribute to the development and production of NASA's Saturn V rockets. (Photograph by J. Allen Hawkins.)

Pictured here in 1959 is the Japan sales representative of the ElectroData division of Burroughs. The sales reps were not the only ones fluent in foreign languages. On June 27, 1957, the company unveiled a prototype system that allowed the computer to translate foreign type into idiomatic English. Programmed by Caltech technician Peter Toma, this was the first computer program that made multiple-language translation possible. (J. Allen Hawkins Collection.)

These men were responsible for the successful 1958 launch of the Explorer I, America's first Earth satellite: Dr. William H. Pickering (left), director of Jet Propulsion Laboratum (JPL), which built and operated the satellite; Dr. James A. Van Allen (center) of the University of Iowa, discoverer of the Van Allen radiation belts that encircle the Earth; and Dr. Werner von Braun, leader of the army's Redstone Arsenal team, which built the satellite's rocket launcher. (*Pasadena Star-News* Collection.)

Herbert Hoover Jr.'s Consolidated Engineering Corporation (founded in 1937) was the first producer of a commercial mass spectrometer, created to analyze gases and light liquids. The CEC mass spectrometer was conceived to revolutionize the way deposits of oil were found underground by locating telltale hydrocarbon gases emanating from below the surface. It took four years and $400,000 to develop. When it was tested, the mass spectrometer did not work as hoped; it never found any underground oil. Nonetheless, it became a sensation in the industry because it could "taste" faint amounts of many substances. Its first job was to find impurities in oil refineries. It quickly became indispensable equipment for the oil industry and was used to help refine improved aviation fuel during World War II. (J. Allen Hawkins Collection.)

Three

SOCIAL STRIFE
AND CHANGE
1960s

By the 1960s, Pasadena was starting to run out of room. Manufacturing businesses seeking to expand began to move their companies elsewhere. A *Los Angeles Times* article from 1962 referred to this as an "industrial exodus," with one firm after another pulling up roots to establish themselves in the cheaper and wider expanses of Fullerton, Santa Ana, and even nearby Monrovia. In the 1940s and 1950s, the last large expanse of undeveloped Pasadena had been developed, and with this industrial exodus, a greater proportion of the tax burden was falling on residents and commercial outlets.

The 1960s was a particularly difficult decade for Pasadena's African Americans. The construction of the 210 and 134 freeways sliced through the historic heart of the African American community. Other neighborhoods, most of them inhabited by nonwhite residents, were also destroyed through massive urban renewal programs.

The civil rights movement in Pasadena was closely connected to the fight for integrated schools. The public schools were highly segregated as a result of housing restrictions that allowed nonwhite residents to live only in certain areas of the city. Angry parents and community members fought for school integration, resulting in the 1967 *Spangler v. the Pasadena Board of Education* court case. In 1970, the California Supreme Court ruled in favor of school integration.

In 1960, the year of this photograph, the Pasadena Merchant's Association celebrated its 64th anniversary. The association had been founded with the primary objective of providing credit ratings for local businesses. Pictured here are the board members and their spouses. Not shown are the organization's 40 employees. (Photograph by Steve Barrett.)

J. Allen Hawkins took this beautiful portrait of All Saints Episcopal Church, located at 132 North Euclid Avenue, on January 15, 1961. The church was founded in 1885 when William and Nellie Vore sold a 62,250-square-foot parcel of land in the San Pascal tract for $750 to All Saints Mission. (J. Allen Hawkins Collection.)

YMCA Christmas tree lots have long been a common sight around the Pasadena area. Here the Foothill Branch of the Pasadena YMCA sells trees outside of a Pancake House on Foothill Boulevard. The 1963 fund-raiser earned money for the construction of a Foothill-area youth headquarters building intended to serve young residents of east Pasadena, Altadena, and Sierra Madre. (J. Allen Hawkins Collection.)

For a time, Pasadena's firemen would select a Miss Firecracker in conjunction with Fourth of July fireworks festivities at the Rose Bowl. This shot is from May 13, 1967, presumably taken before Miss Firecracker was chosen from the group. (J. Allen Hawkins Collection.)

Marvel at the extensive memory units this Burroughs model possesses. The photograph was captured on March 3, 1960. (J. Allen Hawkins Collection.)

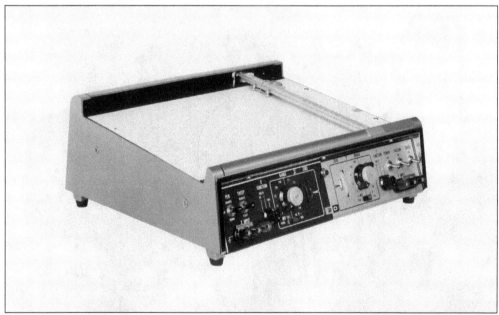

This x-y graphic recorder, produced by the F. L. Moseley Company, was photographed in May 1960. It was precision instruments like this that made Moseley an attractive acquisition for Hewlett Packard. A *Los Angeles Times* piece in October 1960 announced the opening of Moseley's new building at 433 North Fair Oaks Avenue. "Principal products to be manufactured there," the article stated, "include Autograf X-Y and strip chart recorders." (J. Allen Hawkins Collection.)

The Unitarian congregation of Neighborhood Church called this beautiful church at 798 East California Boulevard home in 1951, when this photograph was taken. The congregation formed in 1885 and is today part of the Unitarian Universalist movement. Neighborhood Church is located at 301 North Orange Grove Boulevard, next to Pacific Oaks and the Gamble House. (J. Allen Hawkins Collection.)

The Don Benito Fundamental School (where this photograph was taken in 1966) was established in Upper Hastings Ranch in 1951. The school was named for Benjamin "Don Benito" Wilson, a wealthy landholder and the second mayor of Los Angeles. The boys in the photograph are unidentified. (J. Allen Hawkins Collection.)

George Heussenstamm, William Kraft, and Mrs. F. Bradford Gleason review two musical scores to be performed for the Pasadena Museum of Art's 1969 opening preview party. Kraft and Heussenstamm were commissioned to create special pieces for the occasion; Heussenstamm's "Museum Pieces" and Kraft's "Games: Collage No. 1" were performed by the 26-member Los Angeles Brass and Percussion Ensemble and were conducted by Kraft. (Photograph by Herb Shoebridge, *Pasadena Star-News* Collection.)

The historic Reed House, located in Pasadena's Carmelita Park on the corner of Colorado and Orange Grove Boulevards, was demolished in the mid-1960s to make room for the construction of the Pasadena Art Museum. The museum would become famous for its internationally renowned collection of modern art. (Photograph by Ben Sewell, *Pasadena Star-News* Collection.)

Y. A. and Leonora Curtin Paloheimo stand in their home at 170 North Orange Grove Avenue in June 1961. Y. A. Paloheimo was the Finnish consul for the southwestern United States from 1947 to 1964. In 1970, the Paloheimos donated the home, known today as the Fenyes Mansion (in honor of its original owners), along with its extensive art collection and original furnishings, to the Pasadena Museum of History. (J. Allen Hawkins Collection.)

In 1968, a group of Pasadena's African American residents got together for what they called the Old Timers Picnic. Gatherings of this sort were popular at the time as Pasadena's earlier residents aged and looked back at the many changes that had occurred to both the city and country during their lifetimes. (Black History Collection.)

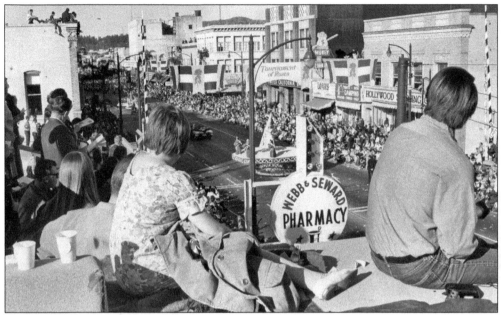

Here people watch the 80th annual Tournament of Rose Parade from the roof of the Webb and Seward Pharmacy, located at 124 East Colorado Boulevard, on January 1, 1969. This parade was one of the warmest on record, with the temperature reaching 80 degrees by the time the parade concluded. More than 1 million people watched the parade in person, and an estimated 65 million watched it on television. (J. Allen Hawkins Collection.)

A representative of the Pasadena Kiwanis poses with the Rose Queen and her court at Tournament House, the Tournament of Rose's headquarters (the former Wrigley Mansion) on Orange Grove Avenue on November 15, 1969. (J. Allen Hawkins Collection.)

Large crowds filled the sidewalks and grandstands along the 1967 Tournament of Rose's parade route. The 1967 parade's grand marshal was Thanat Khoman, Thailand's minister of foreign affairs and the first general marshal selected from outside of the United States. The year's theme was Travel Tales in Flowers, with a larger message of world friendship. (*Pasadena Star-News* Collection.)

Long an essential part of Pasadena's famous Tournament of Roses, the selection and coronation of the Rose Queen and her court is a major event. Here Barbara Hewitt Laughray, age 19, an Altadena resident and Pasadena City College student, is crowned the 1967 Rose Queen. The December 29, 1966, coronation followed a grueling application process that whittled 1,000 local young women down to the queen and her princesses. (*Pasadena Star-News* Collection.)

This is the interior of IBM's Automation Institute at Green Street and Lake Avenue, ordered on behalf of *West Magazine*. J. Allen Hawkins took this photograph on August 8, 1969. (J. Allen Hawkins Collection.)

Since its founding, the intellectual property law firm of Christie, Parker, and Hale has registered patents for hundreds of inventions and important technological innovations that have sprung from the minds of Pasadena's scientific community. This peace sign pretzel, ordered photographed by the firm's Charles Plotner on August 13, 1969, was not one of those. (J. Allen Hawkins Collection.)

Pictured here are the interior and exterior of Vard, Inc., Royal Industries' plant at 2981 East Colorado Boulevard, photographed in December 1963. Vard was a manufacturer of high precision products for the air frame, helicopter, and nuclear engine industries and was acquired by Alhambra-based Royal Industries in 1959. Royal Industries relocated its corporate offices to Pasadena after acquiring Vard, and in 1969, it completed construction on a new headquarters at 980 South Arroyo Parkway. (J. Allen Hawkins Collection.)

J. Allen Hawkins photographed this assortment of testing equipment at the Giannini Controls Monrovia Plant in October 1962. Giannini was doing contract and subcontracting work on large jet and missile projects like the navy's F8U Supersonic Fighter. Giannini Controls became a publicly traded company on April 27, 1960. (J. Allen Hawkins Collection.)

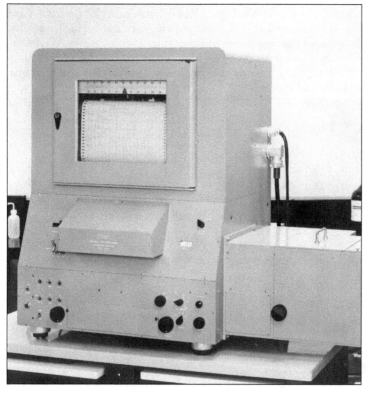

The Applied Physics Corporation was founded in Pasadena in 1946 by Howard Cary, William C. Miller, and George Downs. Cary had previously worked at the National Technology Laboratories for Arnold O. Beckman. Specializing in optical instrumentation, like the recording spectrophotometer pictured here in December 1968, Applied Physics was purchased by Varian Medical Systems in 1966 and became Cary Instruments. In 1958, the company moved to Monrovia. (J. Allen Hawkins Collection.)

Ronald Reagan attended this Pasadena Junior Chamber of Commerce dinner meeting on June 1, 1964. Reagan, seated opposite the speaker and seen in profile, was campaigning for presidential candidate Barry Goldwater. Reagan spoke at the Republican convention that fall, delivering his well-known "Time for Choosing" speech, having rehearsed and refined it over the long campaign season at meetings like this. (J. Allen Hawkins Collection.)

The consummate gentleman and philanthropist, a young Don Fedde shows some of the appliances available for purchase at Fedde Furniture Company in October 1967. Don Fedde had been running the family business since 1963. His parents, Arnold and Ellen, had opened the business in 1937. Don Fedde has served as board president of both the Pasadena Museum of History and the Tournament of Roses. (J. Allen Hawkins Collection.)

The F. L. Moseley Company opened new offices in 1964 at 433 North Fair Oaks Avenue, built by John R. Anderson and Associates using the popular and economical "tilt-up" method, where large concrete slabs are cast on the ground and then tilted into place. In 2006, F. L. Moseley, Inc. completed an award-winning renovation of this building. The building is today home of the Northwest Innovation Center. (J. Allen Hawkins Collection.)

The ElectroData company, minutes from June 22, 1954, state that "Dr. Bacher will be here from Caltech, in the near future; they may want to buy a computer." By the spring of 1960, Caltech was in possession of four computers. The fourth was this Burroughs 220 being test driven by Caltech president Lee DuBridge. It was presented as a gift to Caltech from Burroughs vice president James Bradburn (standing). (J. Allen Hawkins Collection.)

The Stanford Research Institute (SRI) was founded in 1946 by Stanford University and eventually became one of the world's largest independent research organizations. In 1948, SRI opened an outpost in Pasadena. Much of the work conducted by the Southern California SRI team, headed by A. M. Zarem, was experiments relating to air pollution. This photograph shows a July 21, 1969, tour of the Pasadena SRI facility. (J. Allen Hawkins Collection.)

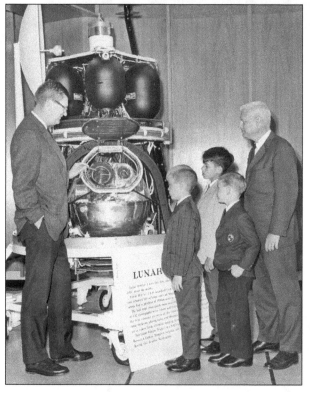

Lunar Orbiter I was the first picture-taking satellite to circle the moon, making the 237,500-mile trip in August 1966. The craft, controlled from JPL, transmitted images of the moon's surface back to earth via radio waves. Scientists were scoping out possible landing sites for the Apollo missions. When Lunar Orbiter I returned to Earth, it was treated with great curiosity. This photograph dates from March 1967. (*Pasadena Star-News* Collection.)

This is the official Pasadena City Board of Directors portrait of Dr. William H. Pickering, taken in March 1968. A native New Zealander, Pickering earned the moniker "Mr. JPL," having served as JPL's fourth and longest-tenured director, from 1954 to 1976. Pickering is one of only a few nonpoliticians to have graced the cover of *Time* twice. (J. Allen Hawkins Collection.)

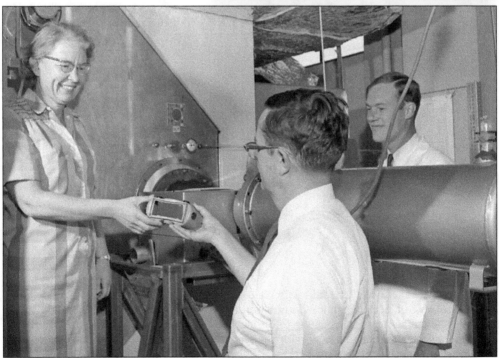

This photograph captures a rather awkwardly staged scene featuring three Pasadena-based Stanford Research Institute employees on August 28, 1968. (Photograph by J. Allen Hawkins.)

J. Allen Hawkins snapped this photograph looking east from Devil's Gate Dam on October 20, 1960. From a similar vantage point in 1916, a writer in the *Los Angeles Times* commented on the scene's mountainous background: "the steep, solid mountains speak of a region of stillness and solitude hidden behind their unwritten sign, 'verboten.'" (J. Allen Hawkins Collection.)

The Consolidated Electrodynamics Corporation merged with Illinois-based Bell and Howell in 1960. The merger was rocky, owing to difficulties in grafting a new corporate culture on CEC, and a general disenchantment with the scientific instrumentation business among Bell and Howell's management. Shown here is a 1961 CEC data tape recorder. In 1969, Bell and Howell sold its CEC division to DuPont Instruments, which dismantled it soon after. (J. Allen Hawkins Collection.)

This is a view of Baker Alley on West Dayton Street, photographed in 1965. Baker Alley was named for John Hamilton Baker, one of Pasadena's original settlers from a group known as the Indiana Colony.

Assembled for this March 30, 1961, photograph are congregants of Scott Methodist Church, a predominantly Filipino church located on Mary Street. (J. Allen Hawkins Collection.)

On display are many models of Mercedes at Lloyd Pearson Studebaker, located at 2025 East Colorado Boulevard. The photograph was taken on April 13, 1961. (J. Allen Hawkins Collection.)

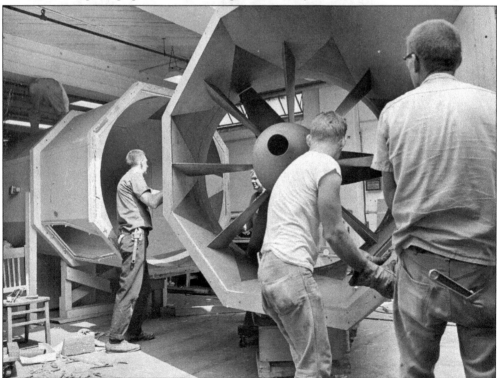

On August 21, 1967, workers dismantled and moved Caltech's Merrill Wind Tunnel into a temporary storage area. The three-bladed fan in the center of the photograph was capable of producing a wind of up to 160 miles per hour. (*Pasadena Star-News* Collection.)

Civil Defense Shelters were popular in October 1961. A note on the reverse of this photograph says that this shelter had been covered and recovered five times. Khrushchev was moving to deny Western access to West Berlin, and in June had threatened "war—and thermonuclear war at that," if the Western powers attempted to force their way into Berlin. (*Pasadena Star-News* Collection.)

Ice-skating legend Peggy Fleming lived and trained for many years in Pasadena before moving to Colorado Springs to train with coach Carlo Fassi during her junior year of high school. She autographed this photograph following her 1968 Olympic gold medal. While in Pasadena, Fleming skated at the Pasadena Winter Garden, located at 171 South Arroyo Parkway.

A fifth grade student poses near Washington Junior High School in Pasadena on August 11, 1969. The photograph was taken to accompany a story about the school desegregation court case *Spangler v. Pasadena Board of Education*, which was being considered by the U.S. Ninth Circuit Court of Appeals at the time. (*Pasadena Star-News* Collection.)

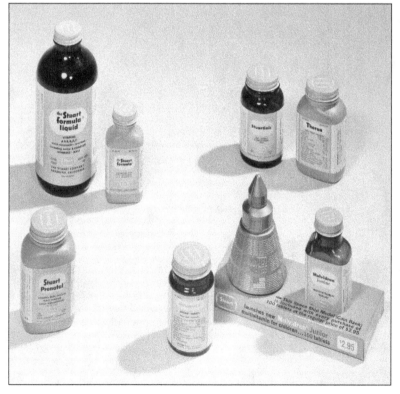

Pasadena's Stuart Company, later Stuart Pharmaceuticals and now part of Astra-Zeneca, was founded in 1941 by bobby sox inventor Arthur Hanisch. Among other things, the Stuart Company produced the world's first stable liquid multivitamin. This photograph was commissioned by the company in January 1964, possibly as part of a patent application. (J. Allen Hawkins Collection.)

Four

URBAN RENEWAL COMES TO TOWN
1970s

The 1970s saw the continuation of urban renewal and change. Pasadena's old commercial heart, then called the Old Town area, was in the midst of its third decade of localized depression. By 1978, though, plans were being developed that would eventually turn old Pasadena's fortunes around, revitalizing the city's tarnished ego at the same time.

As in many other American cities, long-established areas and neighborhoods were demolished and replaced with new developments. Pasadena's historic preservation movement grew in the late 1970s as a direct reaction to this often-destructive approach to urban renewal, with individuals banding together in community groups to prevent the destruction of Pasadena's historic buildings and neighborhoods.

While the results of 1970s-era urban renewal were mixed, the goals were admirable: to provide better housing for local residents and to provide the city with more money and its citizens with more economic opportunity. Large corporations moved their headquarters to the city, millions of square feet of office space were created, and the city's conference center was built.

Substantial inequality in educational opportunities existed between Pasadena's white and minority populations. This led to a landmark court case, *Spangler v. Pasadena Board of Education*, in 1970 that mandated an end to the state of de facto segregation that had come into existence. The decade witnessed a substantial amount of wrangling about bussing and how best to level the academic playing field in the Pasadena Unified School District (PUSD). Many of the scars of this tumultuous period of desegregation and forced bussing are still evident today.

The February 9, 1971, San Fernando earthquake caused significant damage to some Pasadena buildings, including the near-destruction of several churches. The 6.6-magnitude earthquake also left city hall's dome ornament twisted at a 90-degree angle. Shown here is a street scene at Michigan Avenue and Colorado Boulevard following the early morning quake. (*Pasadena Star-News* Collection.)

Dr. Kate Hutton, the "Earthquake Lady," has worked as a seismologist at the California Institute of Technology since the 1970s. Caltech's Seismology Laboratory—unofficially known as the "Seismo Lab"—has been in existence since 1921 and is an important center for the study of earthquakes, both in Southern California and around the world. Dr. Hutton is shown working at the lab in August 1979. (Photograph by Walt Mancini, *Pasadena Star-News* Collection.)

An employee at the Pantry Market, located at 141 South Marengo Avenue, surveys the damage following the February 9, 1971, Sylmar earthquake. (*Pasadena Star-News* Collection.)

Jake's Diner, operating since 1947 at its location at the corner of West Colorado Boulevard and Mills Place, suffered some damage following this April 1978 windstorm. The area around Colorado Boulevard and Fair Oaks Avenue, once Pasadena's core downtown, was in danger of demolition during the 1970s. A group of local activists encouraged the area's revitalization through the preservation of its historic architecture. (Photograph by Brent Sweitzer.)

On October 17, 1972, the center of the partially completed Foothill Freeway Bridge (Interstate 210) tragically collapsed, killing six men and injuring another 21. A 150-foot section of the eight-lane bridge fell 85 feet into the Arroyo Seco below. Here local emergency crews respond to the disaster. (Photograph by Ed Norgord, *Pasadena Star-News* Collection.)

Pasadena's Nash's Department Store, located at 250 East Colorado Boulevard, caught fire in March 1976. Sixty-five firemen from Pasadena and neighboring cities were called upon to fight the three-alarm fire. More than 1 million gallons of water were dumped on the blaze, which started in the first floor hosiery stockroom. Fourteen firemen and one employee suffered injuries, but there were no fatalities. (Photograph by Robert Paz, *Pasadena Star-News* Collection.)

In order to accommodate the new headquarters of the Ralph M. Parsons Company, many homeowners and commercial properties were destroyed. One million dollars were set aside to compensate the 40 families and individuals and 27 businesses that had been occupying the 16-acre site before Parsons began construction. This photograph from January 4, 1973, predates the headquarters' construction. (Photograph by the Ralph M. Parsons Company.)

Contractor William Simpson led the construction of the Ambassador College's Auditorium at 131 South Vernon Avenue, shown here in April 1972. The auditorium became well known for its fine acoustics and played host to more than 2,500 concerts over the years, showcasing a broad range of musical styles. The auditorium was owned by the Worldwide Church of God until 2004, fourteen years after the college's closing. (Photograph by the Transit Mixed Concrete Company.)

Shown here is the United Geophysical's research ship, *UnitedGeo II*, in 1971. The company used such ships to search for oil deposits off the California coast. After placing sensors in the water, an explosive charge was set off underwater, causing sound waves to travel to the ocean bottom. There, reflections from the sea floor were hurled back to the delicate underwater "ears," the results of which signaled oil deposits. (J. Allen Hawkins Collection.)

This is an undersea robot made by the Computer Sciences Corporation (CSC) and photographed in May 1970. CSC was a Century City–based company that was awarded a $4.8 million contract in 1969 to operate a centralized computer facility serving the U.S. Navy's Naval Undersea Warfare Center in Pasadena. (J. Allen Hawkins Collection.)

This is a portrait of Samir Estepan, which was ordered by the Jacobs Engineering Company in September 1970. Jacobs Engineering had grown substantially since its founding in 1947 by Joseph A. Jacobs, the son of uneducated Lebanese immigrants. Today Jacobs Engineering boasts more than $11 billion in annual revenues. (J. Allen Hawkins Collection.)

The Fuller Theological Seminary, shown here in 1977, was founded in 1947. Classes were held at Lake Avenue Congregational Church. In 1952, ground was broken for the construction of a permanent home on Oakland Avenue. The first building housed offices and classrooms and was built for $650,000. Attending the ground-breaking was Dr. Charles E. Fuller, a television evangelist who had made the foundation of the seminary possible with his initial gift. (*Pasadena Star-News* Collection.)

Although a December 30, 1978, article from the *Los Angeles Times* suggested that the odds of surviving a Soviet nuclear attack were "bleak at best," and "fallout shelters of the 1960s are, for the most part, passé, allowed to deteriorate as concern over nuclear attack diminished," this Pasadena Civil Defense Shelter remained well stocked and in apparent good working order. The photograph dates from November 6, 1979. (*Pasadena Star-News* Collection.)

Civil Defense Shelters were designed to keep people safe in the event of a nuclear attack. Emergency communications centers, like this one photographed on November 6, 1979, were also constructed to aid in coordinating responses after an attack. Although the shelters were never needed to protect citizens from atomic fallout, the communications centers were used to handle fires, floods, and earthquakes. (*Pasadena Star-News* Collection.)

Bank of America's five-story building at its Marengo Avenue and Green Street location opened in the 1970s to handle the increasing number of Southern California BankAmericard transactions. Around 1.7 million customers rang up an average of 250,000 sales daily, all processed through new "Data 100" processing technology. The 300,000-square-foot building was more than twice the size of the previous location above Pasadena's main Bank of America office. (*Pasadena Star-News* Collection.)

This photograph was taken on behalf of the Chicago-based Schwinn Bicycle Company at John's Bike Shop, located at 391 South Rosemead Boulevard, on March 26, 1970. (J. Allen Hawkins Collection.)

Christmas decorations are strung across Colorado Boulevard in this photograph, taken on November 28, 1971. The photographer was standing on a roof between Los Robles and Euclid Avenues, facing east. (*Pasadena Star-News* Collection.)

Below is a John Birch Society member, identified as Charles R. Armour, district governor of the 13 Western states for the society and resident of San Marino. Armour and the Birchers were actively involved in linking California senator Alan Cranston with Communist interests and causes around the time when this photograph was taken in 1974. In a Los *Angeles Times* article dated June 24, 1974, a Cranston spokesman referred to the claim as "pure gibberish." (*Pasadena Star-News* Collection.)

Famed inventor Dr. Paul B. MacCready regales a group of Chandler School students in this photograph, taken in November 1979. Yale and Caltech educated, MacCready worked extensively on mechanical contraptions that could function without electric power. His Gossamer Condor and Gossamer Albatross each earned him the prestigious Kremer Prize. The Gossamer Albatross was the first human-powered aircraft to cross the English Channel. MacCready also had a flare for recognizing which budding technologies were ripe for market. In 1971, he founded AeroVironment, a company that developed the EV-1 electric car and drone technology for military use. (*Pasadena Star-News* Collection.)

A team of workers paints the end zone in preparation for a Rose Bowl game in the 1970s. The image is undated, and the knowledge that Ohio State was a participating school does little to help establish the date—Ohio State played in five Rose Bowl games that decade. (*Pasadena Star-News* Collection.)

A group of intrepid Tournament of Roses parade fans camp out along the parade route before the start of the January 1, 1971, Tournament of Roses Parade. (*Pasadena Star-News* Collection.)

The old-time Rose Bowl clock comes down as a new scoreboard sits ready for installation in late 1975. The American Sign and Indicator Company created the solid-state electronic scoreboard for the Rose Bowl. It was installed in time for the Rose Bowl game and what was to have been the stadium's first rock concert, Led Zeppelin, which had to be cancelled because of injuries suffered by Robert Plant in a car accident. (Photograph by Ed Norgord, *Pasadena Star-News* Collection.)

Minnesota Vikings and Oakland Raiders football fans enter the Rose Bowl for Super Bowl XI on January 9, 1977. It was a game filled with firsts: it was the first Super Bowl win for the Raiders, the first half-time show to feature audience participation (people waved colored signs), and the first professional football game played in the Rose Bowl. (Photograph by Robert Paz, *Pasadena Star-News* Collection.)

The year 1978 marked the beginning of a new Pasadena tradition: the irreverent Doo Dah Parade. The first parade was a casual affair with no official marching order or other elements smacking of formality. Joanna Spears of Los Angeles and R. R. Morford of the Pasadena Police Department share a moment during the 1978 parade. (Photograph by Walt Mancini, *Pasadena Star-News* Collection.)

The Doo Dah Parade attracts a broad spectrum of society, giving people platforms to celebrate whatever causes appeals to them (or their sense of humor). In this case, Tom Kelly of Los Angeles exhorts the parade viewers of 1978 to "fight the cover up" by embracing America's nude beaches. (Photograph by Walt Mancini, *Pasadena Star-News* Collection.)

While the Tournament of Roses Parade is never held on a Sunday, the Doo Dah Parade is only scheduled on a Sunday. These marchers kick up their heels at the 1978 Doo Dah Parade. (Photograph by Walt Mancini, *Pasadena Star-News* Collection.)

The Doo Dah Parade's first coroneted queen, Dorothy Ramani, rides with Susan Wilson, her maid-in-waiting, during the 1978 parade. Unlike the Tournament of Roses' strict and traditional queen and royal court requirements, the Doo Dah royalty selection process encourages one and all—regardless of age, gender, or even species—to attend court auditions. (Photograph by Blake Sell, *Pasadena Star-News* Collection.)

Mark Warner sells tickets to the Tournament of Roses Parade in 1977. He had been selling parade tickets at 711 East Colorado Boulevard for each of the previous 25 parades. According to the *Star-News*, the ticket buyer was a man named Ralph Hobin of Sylmar, who said that he would attend the parade rain or shine. Incidentally, it was "shine," as were all Rose Parades between the wet bookends 1955 and 2006. (*Pasadena Star-News* Collection.)

Maria Lynn Caron of La Canada was chosen as the queen of the 89th Tournament of Roses Parade from a field of 907 contestants. Shown here are tryouts in the fall of 1977. The call for contestants demanded that the girls be enrolled in an accredited school in the Pasadena area and wear informal or school attire. Former U.S. president Gerald Ford was the grand marshal of that year's parade. (Photograph by Walt Mancini, *Pasadena Star-News* Collection.)

Pasadenans gathered at Pasadena City Hall's patio on January 27, 1974, to celebrate the 100th anniversary of the formation of the Indiana Colony, the group of settlers generally considered to have founded Pasadena. In another 12 years, residents had the opportunity to celebrate yet again, this time to toast the centennial of the official founding of the city of Pasadena.

The Chandler School was founded in 1950 by Thomas and Catherine Chandler. Originally located in Altadena, the school moved to its permanent home at 1005 Armada Drive in September 1958. This image was copied from a negative in September 1970, possibly to promote the school's 20th anniversary; the original photograph likely dates from the school's Altadena years and features headmaster and founder Thomas Chandler in the back row in a bow tie. (J. Allen Hawkins Collection.)

Arthur Villegas (left) and Gregory White pick up cans of YMCA peanuts from Pasadena's central YMCA, located at 235 East Holly Street, in March 1970. The nuts were part of the YMCA's fund-raising efforts to help children earn money to attend YMCA summer camps. In addition to its summer programs, the YMCA offered many other youth activities. The sign behind the boys advertises a father-son sex education class. (J. Allen Hawkins Collection.)

A brave man streaks through Pasadena City College while bystanders watch with amusement. The year 1974 barely outstrips the competition for year most closely associated with streaking. Not only did a streaker bound across the stage at the Oscars, but a Norman Rockwell commemorative plate featuring his 1921 *Saturday Evening Post* cover, "No Swimming," was advertised thusly: "Certainly 1974 is the year of the streakers! Rockwell immortalizes streaking forever—in the purest commemorative china." (*Pasadena Star-News* Collection.)

Pasadena's Rose Bowl played host to the 1976 World Frisbee Competition, held in August of that year. Shown here is 19-year-old Peter Bloeme of New York. Bloeme won the men's champion title by earning the highest overall score from six categories, including distance, accuracy, and freestyle. Bloeme later won the 1984 Frisbee Dog World Championship with his canine partner Whirlin' Wizard. (Photograph by Vanguard Photography.)

Pasadena Historical Society volunteer docent Nancy Atwell serves lunch at the Fenyes Mansion, a historic house museum open to the public, sometime in the 1970s. The Pasadena Historical Society is now known as the Pasadena Museum of History and is dedicated to the preservation and sharing of the Pasadena area's history and culture. Volunteers continue to lead tours, serve as exhibition gallery hosts, and help out in numerous other ways.

The year 1970 was when Pasadena schools were ordered to desegregate, a result of the court case *Spangler v. Pasadena Board of Education*, though the process was neither smooth nor immediate. This photograph captures the scene after the verdict was read ordering desegregation on March 5, 1970. Each school in the district was not permitted to have a majority of any minority group, something that required extensive bussing to redress. The school board itself sued to overturn aspects of the 1970 decision, and by the time *Spangler v. Pasadena Board of Education* reached the U.S. Supreme Court, several schools were in violation of the original order. In June 1976, the high court overturned the "no majority" clause of the 1970 case. (*Pasadena Star-News* Collection.)

Five

A City Grows Up
1980s

By the 1980s, the destructive tendencies of 1960s- and 1970s-style urban renewal had faded, thanks in part to Pasadena's historic preservation activists. The area around Fair Oaks Avenue and Colorado Boulevard, now known as Old Pasadena, was officially named an Urban Conservation Zone in 1980. Tax incentives encouraged businesses and individuals to invest in the area. In 1983, the Old Pasadena Historic District was added to the National Register of Historic Places. While still seen by many as run-down and gritty, Old Pasadena was no longer at risk for being bulldozed, and the pieces were in place for the gradual renewal and reinvigoration of Pasadena's onetime core downtown.

Some 1980s attempts at urban renewal were not successful. The ill-fated suburban-style enclosed mall, Plaza Pasadena, opened in 1980 on East Colorado Boulevard. Although supporters had high hopes that it would return shoppers to the city's center, the mall ultimately failed.

The 1980s also brought with it a growth in population. The city's population grew by 11 percent between 1980 and 1990. It was also during this decade that the number of Pasadena's Hispanic residents reached almost one-third of the city's overall population. By this time, the city's available space had been fully developed, so rather than building new homes, Pasadena's old and new residents alike turned to already existing neighborhoods. A renewed appreciation for the city's craftsmen homes led to the formation of officially designated historic neighborhoods. Pasadena's Bungalow Heaven led the way and was named the city's first Landmark District in 1989.

This photograph from April 1984 shows the stretch of land where the 710 freeway would meet the 210, if the project were completed. Since 1964, when the plan for the so-called Meridian Avenue route through South Pasadena was adopted, that city has successfully blocked the completion of the final seven "missing link" miles of the 710 freeway (known before October 1985 as California 7). (Photograph by Walt Mancini, *Pasadena Star-News* Collection.)

Throughout the 1980s, Amtrak's *Southwest Chief* ran through Pasadena. Here train attendant Stephen Schweitzer (left) and a City of Pasadena transportation systems management coordinator pose by the new Amtrak traffic signs they helped launch. The station at 222 South Raymond Avenue is visible in the background. Unfortunately for long-distance train travelers, Amtrak's Pasadena service ended in 1994. (Photograph by Walt Mancini, *Pasadena Star-News* Collection.)

Pasadena resident Carle Halford shows off her newly lowered bus fare. When Los Angeles County's Rapid Transit District (RTD) dropped the basic bus fare from 80¢ to 50¢ on July 1, 1982, the transit system's ridership grew dramatically. By October of that year, the RTD was announcing weekday ridership increases of 200,000, as well as large increases of weekend boardings. (Photograph by Ed Norgord, *Pasadena Star-News* Collection.)

Pasadena's Gamble House, an internally renowned example of Arts and Crafts–style architecture, was deeded to the City of Pasadena in 1966. Thousands of visitors tour the house every year, some traveling to California specifically for the purpose. Randell Makinson and James Gamble inspect the new lights in the Gamble House's dining room in March 1988. (*Pasadena Star-News* Collection.)

Pasadena's Elks Lodge is headquartered in this 1911 building located near the intersection of Colorado and Orange Grove Boulevards. Pasadena benefits greatly from this lodge's address; its prime Tournament of Roses viewing location brings it top rental dollars, translating to more funds for the Elks' local charitable projects. Elks Exalted Ruler Al Badger is shown outside the building in 1988. (Photograph by Ed Norgord, *Pasadena Star-News* Collection.)

One of the darkest episodes in Pasadena history centered upon the Lamb Funeral Home. Proprietors Laurieanne and Jerry Sconce and their son David were charged with "sixty-seven criminal offenses, including performing illegal multiple cremations and selling gold fillings and organs from bodies entrusted to their care," according to a *Time* article dated June 6, 1988. The sordid affair resulted in murder and attempted murder charges being brought against David Sconce. (Photograph by Judith Gordon, *Pasadena Star-News* Collection.)

Members of the Old Pasadena Management District bristle when they hear Old Pasadena called Old Town Pasadena. Evidently this large sign near Fair Oaks Avenue and Union Street, photographed in 1985, predates the nomenclatural shift from Pasadena Old Town to Old Pasadena.

The *Pasadena Star-News* announced in May 1986 that a "Pasadena Beautiful Award goes to the home of Garth and Christle Hintz along with their daughter Dhari and the dog Wiley." Pasadena Beautiful was founded in 1960 to provide a uniting and implementing force for the efforts of individuals and groups toward city beautification. (Photograph by Ed Norgord, *Pasadena Star-News* Collection.)

The Avery Dennison headquarters (then Avery International) at 150 North Orange Grove Boulevard was selected to receive a 1986 Pasadena Beautiful Award for Landscape Excellence. "One is struck by the fact that a commercial building does not have to reflect a sterile image," raved the Pasadena Beautiful Foundation. "The grounds flow into those of the neighboring Historical Society, a blending of old and new Pasadena landmarks." (*Pasadena Star-News* Collection.)

The Pasadena Showcase Home, one of the nation's largest and most financially successful home and garden tours, started as a fund-raiser for musical nonprofits and causes in 1948. David Galvery decorated this "Sultan's Chamber" for the 1984 Pasadena Showcase Home. Sitting on the bed is Fran Benuska, the chairman of the Pasadena Junior Philharmonic Committee. (*Pasadena Star-News* Collection.)

Pasadena's First Church of Christ, Scientist, located at the corner of Green Street and Oakland Avenue, is a local landmark. The 1910 building's distinctive dome was the first ever to be built of reinforced concrete. Here it gets some fresh paint in March 1987. Twenty years later, in 2007, the church and its historic dome completed an 18-month restoration that included, among other things, seismic retrofitting and electrical upgrades.

The Whittier Narrows earthquake of October 1, 1987, struck at 7:42 in the morning. School had already started at Pasadena's Jefferson Elementary School. Here students and teachers waited for parents to arrive in the outdoor safety of Jefferson Park, located across from the Villa Street school. (Photograph by Ed Norgord, *Pasadena Star-News* Collection.)

Earthquakes are a part of life for residents of Southern California. The Whittier Narrows earthquake, a 5.9-magnitude earthquake with an epicenter in nearby Rosemead, destroyed more than 10,000 buildings in the region. These cars were crushed under the collapsed building at 101 South Fair Oaks Avenue in Old Pasadena. (Photograph by John Lloyd, *Pasadena Star-News* Collection.)

The State Theater at 770 E.
Colorado Boulevard, opened in 1918,
went through many incarnations
before closing in 2000. When this
photograph was taken on August
29, 1989, the theater was playing
old favorites from Hollywood's past.
After closing its ticket booth for good,
the theater was converted to retail
use. (Photograph by Nelson Green,
Pasadena Star-News Collection.)

Pasadena's Colorado Street Bridge, spanning the banks of the Arroyo Seco, has gained an
unfortunate reputation as a destination for would-be suicide jumpers. Suicide barriers were installed
during a 1993 renovation of the bridge and have since deterred some, although not all, jumpers.
In this photograph, police help a man down from the railing in 1988 after talking him out of
taking his life. (Photograph by Paul Morse, *Pasadena Star-News* Collection.)

JPL was abuzz in August 1981 as Voyager II was nearing and then passing Saturn. The Voyager-Saturn rendezvous caused another significant confluence, an unprecedented meeting of three Caltech presidents. From left to right are Dr. Harold Brown (1969–1977), Dr. Lee DuBridge (1946–1968), and then-president Dr. Marvin Goldberger (1978–1987.). Missing is Dr. Robert F. Christy, who was acting president (1977–1978) between the tenures of Brown and Goldberger. (*Pasadena Star-News* Collection.)

Pictured here is a horse and rider at the Eaton Canyon Riding Club on November 15, 1987. Although Pasadena is a city, its proximity to the foothills and its many parks—including that of Eaton Canyon—give local residents plentiful opportunities to experience nature. (Photograph by M. Weikert, *Pasadena Star-News* Collection.)

Robert F. Christy contributed enormously to the Manhattan Project's theoretical division. The plutonium implosion device tested at Alomogordo, New Mexico, on July 16, 1945, is known as the "Christy Gadget" or "Christy Bomb." This test was the world's first atomic explosion. After the war, Christy joined Caltech's staff, replacing Robert Oppenheimer, whom Christy had studied under at Berkeley. Today Christy is an emeritus professor. (J. Allen Hawkins Collection.)

This photograph was taken at the Jet Propulsion Laboratory in 1968 during a ceremony commemorating Frank Malina's rocket experiments. Malina (pictured here, at left, with Caltech president Lee DuBridge, center, and JPL director William Pickering) was one of GALCIT's rocket pioneers, a founder of the Aerojet Corporation, and the JPL's first director. This photograph appeared in the November 11, 1981, *Los Angeles Times* article announcing Malina's death. (*Pasadena Star-News* Collection.)

This is a photograph of the first annual Peace Sunday, an interfaith event held to support the Second Session of the United Nations on Disarmament and its goal of working toward eventual global nuclear disarmament. Approximately 85,000 participants attended the June 1982 event at the Rose Bowl. (Photograph by John Lloyd, *Pasadena Star-News* Collection.)

Workers as Pasadena's Rose Bowl laid a new sod field in June 1984 in preparation for that year's summer Olympic Games. The Rose Bowl hosted soccer events, and the unexpected crowds—more than 90,000 people attended each game—showed the world that Americans were ready to embrace soccer. Ten years later, the Rose Bowl hosted North America's first World Cup. (Photograph by Walt Mancini, *Pasadena Star-News* Collection.)

A blimp draws a large happy face in the sky above the 1987 Super Bowl. Super Bowl XXI was the fourth of five times the Rose Bowl has played host to a Super Bowl game. The other Super Bowl years were 1977, 1980, 1983, and 1993. The only other stadiums that have hosted as many Super Bowls are the Miami Orange Bowl (five) and the Louisiana Superdome (six). (Photograph by Walt Mancini, *Pasadena Star-News* Collection.)

Here Denver Broncos fans prepare for Super Bowl XXI at their campsite in Brookside Park. They are cheering, drinking, and cranking a siren. The Broncos fell to the New York Giants 39-20. (Photograph by John Lloyd, *Pasadena Star-News* Collection.)

More than 10,000 Pasadena residents attended the city's June 1986 Centennial Celebration to listen to speeches, pose for an official city photograph, eat cake, and release birthday balloons. "Pasadena is not [just] a city," said celebration chairwoman Carolyn Carlburg. "It's a state of mind." "This afternoon has been fun, hasn't it?" Mayor John Crowley asked the crowd. "That's the spirit of Pasadena." (Photograph by Ed Norgord, *Pasadena Star-News* Collection.)

What celebration is complete without a cake? Official Pasadena centennial cake sponsor Bill Podley poses next to the cake top with Kari Sperry of Takes the Cake Bakery in June 1986. The 10-foot-wide cake used 80 gallons of batter and served up a half million calories. It was frosted in the official centennial colors of teal, lavender, and magenta. (Photograph by Judith Gordon, *Pasadena Star-News* Collection.)

Radio station KABC's *Ken and Bob Show* sponsored an official Pasadena centennial song contest in commemoration of the city's 1986 Centennial Celebration. Mario Jojola (left) and Jeff Platt won first place with "Not Just Another Pretty Face," a country-style song that won the duo a trip to Pasadena, Texas, and an evening at Gilley's nightclub. The city's official song remains "Home in Pasadena." (Photograph by John Lloyd, *Pasadena Star-News* Collection.)

Mark Hilbert stands outside of his Singer Building in September 1981. The building, on the corner of East Colorado Boulevard and Oakland Avenue, was built in 1926 by the Singer Sewing Company to serve as its West Coast headquarters. Designed by Everett Phipps Babcock, who worked in Wallace Neff's office, the building was restored by Hilbert. (*Pasadena Star-News* Collection.)

This is the South Lake parking lot between Cordova and San Pasqual Streets. The photograph was taken by Walt Mancini from the Howe Building, located at 180 South Lake Avenue at Del Mar Boulevard, looking south toward San Pasqual Street in 1985. Ample parking helped make the South Lake District a preferred destination of Pasadena shoppers. (Photograph by Walt Mancini, *Pasadena Star-News* Collection.)

Six

REVITALIZATION AND GROWTH
1990s

The 1990s saw major changes in Old Pasadena, the district surrounding the Colorado Boulevard and Fair Oaks Avenue intersection in Pasadena's historic downtown. Although saved from the demolition-as-renewal policies of the 1970s, the district was still seen by many as seedy and run-down. An ambitious project integrating the area's historic architecture into a newly reenergized shopping and dining district culminated in the opening of the award-winning One Colorado project in 1994. Other projects and building restorations quickly followed, and by the end of the decade, Old Pasadena was on its way to a restored status as Pasadena's main business, retail, and dining district.

Pasadena's city government changed from a board of directors to a city council during the 1990s, a change designed, in part, to increase minority representation and to better address neighborhood issues.

The Tournament of Roses continued to be a major force in Pasadena life, with the annual January parade and Rose Bowl game attracting visitors from around the world. In 1994, the Rose Bowl Stadium also hosted the final game of the World Cup, a milestone event that marked the first time the World Cup was held in North America.

By the 1990s, historic preservation was firmly entrenched in Pasadena, with many local residents and politicians seeing its value for both the city's quality of life as well as for the accompanying economic benefits. In 1993, Pasadena completed a seismic retrofit of the 1913 Colorado Street Bridge, a sign of the city's dedication to preserving its past for the benefit of the future.

Animals and humans joined together in 1994 to celebrate the opening of the remodeled Pasadena Humane Society. Participants in this "ribbon-eating ceremony" included Rocky (left), a drug-detecting dog in the Pasadena Police Department's canine unit; K. J. (center); and Charlie. The dogs chewed their way through ceremonial bones while Pasadena police officer Joe Allard held one end of the ribbon and Pasadena Humane Society director Steve McNall held the other. (*Pasadena Star-News* Collection.)

These young coyotes became a point of citywide controversy in May 1991 after 2 of the 10 pups were trapped and shot at the Brookside Golf Course. The coyotes were using the course's drainage ditches as a personal transportation network. Ultimately the Pasadena Humane Society removed the two dens and their occupants. (Photograph by Nancy Newman, *Pasadena Star-News* Collection.)

According to the *Pasadena Star-News*, pictured is "Bobby Fine [using] binoculars to get a closer look on mischief in the Arroyo," on March 24, 1990. The police department had created a volunteer mounted unit to aid in patrolling during the 1984 Olympics, and the unit was formalized and adopted in 1985. (Photograph by Paul Morse, *Pasadena Star-News* Collection.)

Jesus Avon, Jill Polsby, and Alice Kennedy plant the 200th tree in the Pasadena Beautiful Foundation's Pasadena Street Trees project on South Arroyo Boulevard on December 8, 1994. The foundation's mission is to protect and enhance Pasadena's urban forest and streetscape by encouraging beautification and sustainable landscapes, both public and private. (Photograph by Michael Haering, *Pasadena Star-News* Collection.)

The main entrance and lobby of this new Huntington Hospital building, located at 100 West California Boulevard, was photographed in November 1990 shortly before its December opening. The building's 222,000 square feet and three floors held the emergency room and the trauma center, among other things. (Photograph by Walt Mancini, *Pasadena Star-News* Collection.)

Kirk Downey of the Taxpayers Coalition Against Proposition 187 speaks to Pasadena teens in October 1994. Students threatened to walk out of school to protest the Proposition; many did. There were also many protests around the city. Extremely controversial, Proposition 187 was also known as the "Save Our State" initiative, and sought to bar illegal immigrants from accessing social services, public education, or health care. (*Pasadena Star-News* Collection.)

Photographed on February 16, 1995, are customers enjoying coffee at Starbucks in the newly built shopping center that includes Ralphs Grocery Market in the lower Hasting Ranch area of Pasadena. (Photograph by Walt Mancini, *Pasadena Star-News Collection*.)

Heidi Fleiss, the notorious Hollywood madam, brought her business—no, not *that* business—to Pasadena when she opened a shop on Colorado Boulevard in Old Pasadena. During the mid-1990s, one could purchase sweatshirts, boxers, T-shirts, and other goods at Heidi Wear and get them autographed on the spot by Fleiss herself. She closed the store in 1996 following her conviction for tax evasion. (Photograph by Michael Haering, *Pasadena Star-News* Collection.)

In 1994, soccer's World Cup came to the United States for the first time. Although the location was officially Los Angeles, many of the games—including the final match—were actually held in Pasadena's Rose Bowl. Here Pasadena police chief Jerry Oliver (left) and police investigator John Perez pose for an official *Pasadena Star-News* photograph designed to point out the disparity. (Photograph by Michael Haering, *Pasadena Star-News* Collection.)

Soccer fans celebrate the United States' 2-1 win over Columbia in the 1994 World Cup. Nearly 94,000 fans had watched the match at the Rose Bowl, and these revelers had made their way to Old Pasadena to continue the celebration. (Photograph by Scott Quintard, *Pasadena Star-News* Collection.)

This July 1993 photograph shows a pack of high-speed bikers on Seco Street near the Rose Bowl. The local roads have long attracted top bikers from around the country. There have been many discussions over the years about whether to ban bikes and cars from area streets, but for now bikes, pedestrians, and cars continue to try to safely and respectfully share the space. (*Pasadena Star-News* Collection.)

J. P. Henderson (left), a volunteer for the Eaton Canyon Recovery Alliance, and Michael Antonovich, Los Angeles County supervisor, dig a hole to plant a tree at Eaton Canyon Nature Center on October 27, 1994. The tree is a native Fremont Cottonwood. It was planted in remembrance of the previous year's fire that destroyed the nature center. (Photograph by Walt Mancini, *Pasadena Star-News* Collection.)

This 1994 photograph documents early construction on Pasadena's light rail line. The exact route and line went through various incarnations, with potential names at one time including both the Blue Line (now built elsewhere) and the Rose Line, in honor of Pasadena's Tournament of Roses heritage. Officials finally settled on the Gold Line name. (Photograph by Ralph Melching.)

During the 1994 bus strike, the Metropolitan Transportation Authority contracted school buses to transport riders. Here passengers board a bus at a stop on Los Robles Avenue near Colorado Boulevard. (Photograph by Walt Mancini, *Pasadena Star-News* Collection.)

Students from Pasadena High School joined together to raise money and collect food for the victims of the June 1992 Los Angeles riots. From left to right are teacher Ash Vasudeva and student club representatives Paul Boghospatatian, Monica Madan, Jeannine Guana, Kate Bond, and Kareen Kjestrom. Collectively the student body raised $500 and 400 cans of food for the cause. (Photograph by Matthew Ho, *Pasadena Star-News* Collection.)

The Chuang family of Pasadena poses here with their Chinese New Year decorations in January 1995. Although Pasadena's Chinese connections date to the 19th century, it was during the 1990s that Pasadena's and the San Gabriel Valley's Chinese American populations exploded. Today the city is home to Chinese Americans as well as recent immigrants from China, Taiwan, and Hong Kong. (Photograph by Michael Haering, *Pasadena Star-News* Collection.)

Presidential visits have been regular occurrences throughout Pasadena's history, and they never fail to provoke a response—both positive and negative—among local residents. In 1991, these pro-choice protesters staged this protest at Caltech around the time of U.S. president George Bush's 1991 commencement address at the school. (Photograph by Jonathan Alcorn, *Pasadena Star-News* Collection.)

Walt Mancini captured this humorous, impromptu "Outside World" sign on the Caltech grounds on December 13, 1991. Caltech students are famous for their sense of humor, which often results in elaborate pranks and competitions with rival Massachusetts Institute of Technology (MIT). (Photograph by Walt Mancini, *Pasadena Star-News* Collection.)

Pasadena's Jewish Temple and Center, located at 1434 North Altadena Drive, was originally founded in 1923 as the Temple B'Nai Israel. In the 1940s, the temple was moved to its current location and changed its name to acknowledge its larger role as both a temple and a community center. Here Rabbi Gilbert Kollin holds a torah in preparation for Yom Kippur in 1990. (Photograph by Nancy Newman, *Pasadena Star-News* Collection.)

Robert Baderian, director of the Pasadena Recreation and Parks Department, poses with Patricia Knudsen, executive director of the Pasadena Senior Center, in November 1994. The site behind them was slated as the location of the center's planned expansion, which was completed in 1998. (Photograph by Michael Haering, *Pasadena Star-News* Collection.)

Parents, students, and community members protested violence and low academic achievement at Muir High School in Pasadena in February 1995. Donna Wells Smith holds the large sign; her daughter was an 11th grader at the school. (Photograph by Walt Mancini, *Pasadena Star-News* Collection.)

Radical P.A.S.T., Contemporary Art in Pasadena, 1961–1974, was an exhibition in three parts. Norton Simon, the Art Center College of Design, and the Armory Center for the Arts each hosted exhibits that celebrated the era when the Pasadena Art Museum flourished and featured works by many extraordinary 20th century artists. This installation at the Art Center displayed paintings by (from left to right) Roy Lichtenstein, Kenneth Noland, and Robert Morris. (Installation view, *Radical Past: Influences*, 1999; Alyce de Roulet Williamson Gallery, Art Center College of Design.)

Seven

MODERN PASADENA
2000s

The 2000s has been, for the most part, a good decade for Pasadena. Continued revitalization has boosted the city's downtown. Old Pasadena has become a regional draw, attracting both locals and visitors alike to its many shops and restaurants. Businesses maintain offices in the area, and new residential developments bring even more downtown activity. Farther down Colorado Boulevard, the 2003 Paseo Colorado project opened up the former Plaza Pasadena mall to the street, energizing the area and providing an economic boost to the Playhouse District. South Lake Avenue is home to many banks and office buildings, and the historic Bullock's Department Store—now Macy's—recently underwent a renovation. Other revitalization efforts include the growth of the heavily Armenian East Washington Avenue neighborhood and its commercial district.

Another major development in Pasadena during the 2000s was the opening of the Gold Line, a light rail line connecting Pasadena with downtown Los Angeles and beyond. Pasadena's six stations opened in 2003.

Arts and culture remain an integral part of Pasadena's community life. The city's popular ArtNight events provide free admission to many of the city's museums, galleries, and theaters, ensuring that all residents, regardless of income, have access to the city's significant cultural amenities.

While Pasadena's economy was strong for most of the 2000s, it, like the rest of the United States, began to face difficulties toward the end of the decade. In July 2008, the city made national news when Pasadena-based IndyMac Bank became the United States' second largest bank failure to date.

This photograph was taken at the 2007 No Boundaries show, which was held at the Homestead House at 680 East Colorado Boulevard. Winning art pieces from this year's show were later displayed at city hall. In March 2009, the fourth installment of No Boundaries was held on South Lake Avenue. (Photograph by Joan Palmer.)

Art and Ideas is a citywide cultural partnership organized by the Pasadena Arts Council. In 2007, the collaboration was entitled SKIN, and each of the festival's 22 participants interpreted that according to their institutional focus. Pictured here is Dinh Q. Lee's *Untitled (Persistence of Memory #17)*. This piece of artwork was part of the exhibition *New Images of Identity* presented by the Armory Center for the Arts. (Shoshana Wayne Gallery.)

The oldest art service organization in California, the Pasadena Arts Council (founded in 1964) offers an independent voice for promoting a vibrant cultural community by facilitating, empowering, and advocating for the arts. One of its programs is the Next Step, an after-school program at John Muir High School that provides students (like the one pictured here) with an in-depth understanding of music, television, and film production.

Shown here are visitors to the 2008 No Boundaries show jointly sponsored by the Pacific Asia Museum and the Pasadena Museum of California Art. Also supported by the Pasadena Unified School District (PUSD) and the city's Arts and Culture Commission is the My Masterpieces program linking Pasadena's word-class arts and culture organizations with PUSD classrooms. (Photograph by Joan Palmer.)

The City of Pasadena enjoys many wonderful pieces of public art, which are administered by the city's Cultural Affairs Division. This dramatic intaglio carving is on the Montana's facade over the building's main entrance at 345 East Colorado Boulevard. Titled *Raptor Intaglio* and carved by artist Gwynn Murrill in 2008, the artwork is approximately 16 feet tall and 22 feet wide. (Gwynn Murrill Studios.)

The No Boundaries program was created in 2006 to display artwork from across the Pasadena Unified School District at the Art Center College of Design's South Campus during ArtNight, a twice-yearly event sponsored by the city's Arts and Culture Commission, where partnering cultural organizations open their doors for free to the public. This is one of the student art pieces from the 2007 show. (Photograph by Joan Palmer.)

No Boundaries encompasses performing arts as well as the visual arts. In 2008, students performed music, dance, and dramatic pieces against the backdrop of the student artwork. (Photograph by Joan Palmer.)

One piece of public art that has been recently completed is *Bighorn Fountain*, by Gwynn Murrill, which sits on the property of the Montana, a mixed-use development at 345 East Colorado Boulevard. The statue of a San Gabriel Mountain bighorn sheep sits in the foreground of the recently renovated city hall. *Bighorn Fountain* was produced in 2008. (Gwynn Murrill Studios.)

Siblings Mira Conyers (age 10) and Leo Conyers (age 2) enjoy an unfamiliar scene, a rainy day in Pasadena, in November 2008. (Photograph by Patrick Conyers.)

In 2006, the Pasadena Museum of History hosted the traveling Smithsonian exhibition Doodles, Drafts, and Designs: Industrial Drawings from the Smithsonian. Local intellectual property law firm Christie, Parker, and Hale sponsored the exhibition. Pasadena has long been a hotbed of innovation, and one of its most celebrated inventors was Dr. Paul A. MacCready (1925–2007), who delivered a keynote lecture in conjunction with the exhibition. (Photograph by Diane Siegel.)

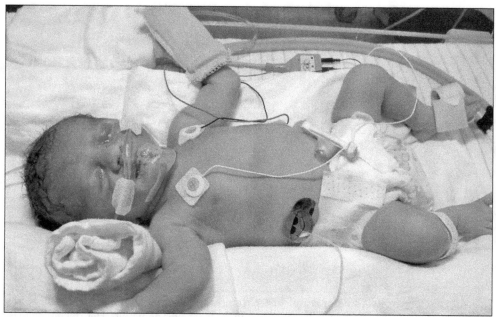

Huntington Hospital's neonatal intensive care unit (NICU) is a level III facility, meaning that it is equipped to care for the most premature of babies or those with other severe problems. Jackson Phillips was photographed shortly after his unexpected and early July 2007 birth. Delivered nearly seven weeks early, Phillips spent two weeks in one of Huntington Hospital's 51 NICU beds. (Cedar Phillips.)

These renderings of the Paseo Colorado Project, located on the site of the former Plaza Pasadena Mall on Colorado Boulevard, show the architect's vision of a retail, dining, and residential complex that retains some elements of the traditional mall but opens it up to both the street and to the sky. Paseo Colorado opened in 2001 and successfully markets itself as an "urban village."

The Tournament of Roses Foundation, the philanthropic arm of the Tournament of Roses organization, funnels thousands of dollars each year to Pasadena-area nonprofits. Here representatives from organizations receiving grants in 2007 pose on the steps of the Tournament of Rose's Orange Grove headquarters. Since its funding in 1983, the Tournament of Roses Foundation had contributed more than $1.9 million to a broad range of organizations providing a diverse array of social and cultural services to the residents of Pasadena and neighboring communities. (Tournament of Roses Foundation.)

On October 27, 2006, then Illinois senator Barack Obama was a guest on *AirTalk with Larry Mantle*. Obama visited the KPCC studios to promote his new book, *The Audacity of Hope*, and to answer Mantle's questions. *AirTalk* first aired on 89.3 KPCC on April 1, 1985, and has played a leading role in shaping the civic discourse in Southern California for almost 25 years. Pasadena-based KPCC, the flagship station of Southern California Public Radio, has won more awards for excellence in journalism this decade than any other radio station in Southern California. KPCC produces two, two-hour call-in shows that air each weekday (*AirTalk* and *Patt Morrison*), as well as *Off-Ramp with John Rabe*, a weekly show of Southern California cultural miscellany. (Photograph by Bill Youngblood.)

ABOUT THE MUSEUM

The Pasadena Museum of History, first founded in 1924 as the Pasadena Historical Society, is dedicated to sharing and preserving the history, art, and culture of Pasadena and its neighboring communities. The museum's campus, located at the corner of Orange Grove Boulevard and Walnut Street, includes the modern History Center, the historic Fenyes Mansion, the Finnish Folk Art Museum, and the Curtin House. The History Center is home to exhibition space, administrative offices, collections storage spaces, and the only library and archives in the world dedicated solely to Pasadena area history and culture. The Fenyes Mansion is operated as a historic house museum and is open for docent-led tours. More information about the Pasadena Museum of History, including current hours, exhibitions, and educational program listings, can be found online at www.pasadenahistory.org or by calling (626) 577-1660.

Visit us at
arcadiapublishing.com

Printed in the USA
CPSIA information can be obtained
at www.ICGtesting.com
LVHW010313311023
762642LV00006B/40